DRUG CRIME

Dirk Flint

W

FRANKLIN WATTS
LONDON • SYDNEY

First published in 2010 by
Franklin Watts
338 Euston Road
London NW1 3BH

Franklin Watts Australia
Level 17/207 Kent Street
Sydney NSW 2000

Series editor: Jeremy Smith
Editors: Sarah Ridley and Julia Bird
Design: sprout.uk.com
Artworks: sprout.uk.com
Picture research: Diana Morris

A CIP catalogue record for this book is available
from the British Library.

ISBN 978 0 7496 9583 5

Dewey classification: 364.1'77

Printed in China

Franklin Watts is a division of Hachette Children's
Books, an Hachette UK company.
www.hachette.co.uk

Picture credits: AFP/Getty Images: 20. Paula
Bronstein/Getty Images: 14, 17, 38. Andrew Burns/
Shutterstock: front cover c. Canadian Press/Rex
Features: 33. Michael Cogliantry/Getty Images:
29. Scott Dalton/Bloomberg/Getty Images: 37.
Keith Dannemiller/Alamy: 39t. Peter Dazeley/Getty
Images: 24. DEA/AP/PAI: 21. DEA/Corbis: 35.
Mauricio Duenas/AFP/Getty Images: 22. Alfredo
Estrella/AFP/Getty Images: 13. Romeo Gacad/
AFP/Getty Images: 15. Paul Gilham/Getty Images:
30. terry harris just greece photolibrary/Alamy: 40.
David Hoffman/Alamy: 41. Mario Laporta/AFP/Getty
Images: 5, 25. Ho New/Reuters: 34. Guang Nui/
Getty Images: 39b. Andrea Pistolesi/Getty Images:
28. Joe Raedle/Getty Images: front cover b. Paul
Rapson/SPL: 31. John Robertson/Alamy: 16. Rafa
Salafranca/epa/Corbis: 19, 27. Alexei Sazonov/
AP/PAI: 11b. Antonio Scorza/AFP/Getty Images: 9.
Sipa Press/Rex Features: 8, 12, 23. Omar Torres/
AFP/Getty Images: 26. US Coastguard: 18. Walik/
istockphoto: front cover t. Wallenrock/Shutterstock:
10. Janine Wiedel Photolibrary/Alamy: 32.

Every attempt has been made to clear copyright.
Should there be any inadvertent omission, please
apply to the publisher for rectification.

CONTENTS

Drug crime:
  a worldwide problem 8

Which drugs are illegal? 10

Who are the criminals? 12

The flow of drugs 14

The cost of drugs 16

Tackling the traffickers 18

Smuggling and mules 20

Case study: Below the waves! 22

Stop and search 24

Global drug watch 26

Surveillance 28

Case study:
  Operation Junglefowl 30

Going undercover 32

The bust 34

Case study: Operation Habitat 36

Rehabilitation 38

The future 40

Glossary 42

Further information 43

Index 44

DRUG CRIME: A WORLDWIDE PROBLEM

Illegal drugs bring problems, not just to the person who takes the drugs but to the communities where the drugs are grown or produced, trafficked and sold. The international community spends a great deal of time and money working out how to fight drug crime in all its forms.

Legal and illegal drugs

A drug is any substance that affects the body. Throughout history, governments have decided which drugs will be legal and which illegal in their own country. Tobacco and alcohol are legal drugs in most countries whilst drugs such as heroin, cocaine, amphetamines and cannabis are illegal. Punishments for producing, selling or handling illegal drugs vary around the world.

▼ Drug users taking cocaine in Colombia. The drug is linked to gang crime across Colombia, and worldwide.

The criminals

Because certain drugs are illegal, there is a huge amount of money to be made in smuggling them across national borders and into the countries where they can be sold at high prices. Drug traffickers work in great secrecy to produce and transport these illegal drugs. As ruthless as they are organised, they think nothing of murdering anyone who gets in their way. Other drug-related criminal offences include possessing illegal drugs and selling them on.

The war on drugs

Over 40 years have passed since US President Nixon declared 'a war on drugs' in 1969, but criminals are making more profit than ever. Law enforcement agencies seize only a small proportion of the tonnes of heroin and cocaine produced each year. Police officers continue to battle drug crime on the streets by arresting drug users and tackling drug-related crime. But is there a better way to combat drug crime? Some argue that making drugs legal will stop money getting into the hands of criminal gangs. Others believe it will simply make it easier for people to get hold of dangerous drugs that can destroy the lives of users and those around them.

▲ Military Police in Rio de Janeiro, Brazil, arrest members of two drug gangs, the Comando Vermelho and the Terceiro Comando.

THE WORLD OF DRUGS

MAIN PROBLEM DRUGS FOR COUNTRIES ACROSS THE WORLD,
AS REFLECTED IN TREATMENT PROVIDED

The annual World Drug Report 2009, published by the United Nations Office on Drugs and Crime, shows the size of the world's drug problem. In 2007:

• up to 190 million people used cannabis

• up to 51 million people took amphetamines

• up to 23 million people took ecstasy

• up to 21 million people took opiates, such as heroin

• up to 20 million people took cocaine

• between 18-38 million people were heavy drug users and addicts.

Proportion of drug users in the world
People aged 15-64

4,343m
(All people aged 15-64 in 2007)

250m — *Number who have used drugs once in the past year*
38m — *Problem drug users*
21m — *Number who inject drugs*

Total users
Numbers of people

190m
50m
23m
21m
20m

■ Opiates
□ Cannabis
■ Cocaine
■ Amphetamines
■ Ecstasy
□ Others
□ No data

WHICH DRUGS ARE ILLEGAL?

Drugs are part of our everyday lives. Many people rely on legal medicinal drugs to keep them well or to treat illnesses. But some drugs can be dangerous to people's health. That's why drugs such as ecstasy, cocaine and heroin are illegal. Drug abuse can lead to illness or death, and is linked to a range of crimes from theft to murder. Over the past 100 years, it has become a crime to use or sell such drugs in just about every country in the world.

What is a drug?

A drug is any chemical that has an effect on your body, often changing the way you feel or act. Many drugs are safe. Chocolate, coffee and tea, for instance, all contain the legal drug caffeine. This can give a mild 'buzz' and a short burst of energy. In fact, coffee was banned in some Middle Eastern countries during the 16th century for being too stimulating. Other legal drugs, such as alcohol or the nicotine in cigarettes, help people relax. Though it is legal to consume these drugs, they still have to be used with care. It is against the law to use or sell drugs such as cocaine and heroin, mainly because they are so addictive.

◄ Nicotine, the drug in tobacco, is highly addictive. It takes great willpower to stop smoking once it has become a habit.

FACT FILE

Tobacco and alcohol kill far more people than cocaine and heroin. Smokers are much more likely to develop cancer, heart disease or other breathing illnesses. Drinking alcohol can damage internal organs as well as affecting memory and mental health. Alcohol is linked to the development of several different cancers. Of course, it is worth noting that both these drugs are widely available, unlike illegal drugs.

- In the United Kingdom, on average 3,000 people are killed or seriously injured each year in drink-drive accidents. Over 1,000 children under the age of 15 go to hospital each year with severe alcohol poisoning.

- In the United States, tobacco kills about 450,000 people a year, alcohol kills about 85,000, while illegal drugs kill less than 20,000 people.

- Over the past few years, smoking in public places has been banned in a growing number of countries. This is due to the damage caused by passive smoking – breathing in the smoke from someone else's cigarette.

Dangerous drugs

One of the oldest drugs still in use is opium, which is made from the seeds of the opium poppy. Though it can be used as a powerful painkiller, it also affects people's minds. The drug heroin is made from morphine, the active ingredient in opium. It tricks the brain into feeling good. Some drugs, such as cocaine and amphetamines, make the user feel alert and full of energy. Hypnotic drugs, such as cannabis, make the user feel calm, while LSD changes the way users see or hear things. Some of these feelings, however, can turn to desperate cravings. More and more of the drug is needed for the same effect. The chemical balance in the brain is affected, so the user finds it hard to cope without the drug's effect.

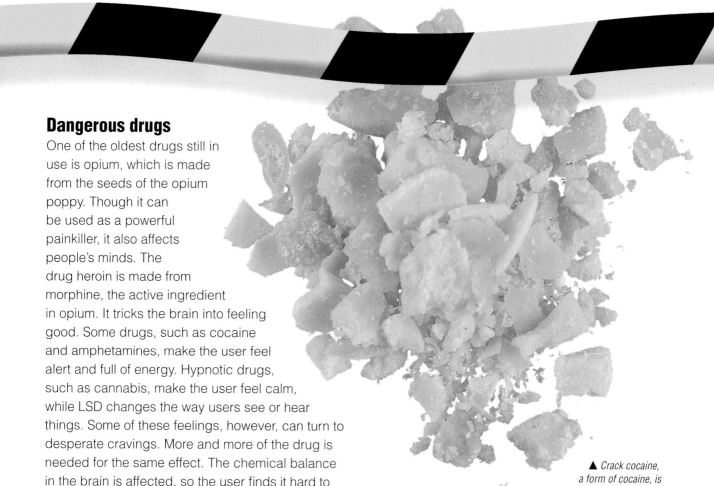

▲ Crack cocaine, a form of cocaine, is extremely addictive and has been linked to many deaths from overdoses.

Drug types

In the UK, illegal drugs are divided into three groups. Class A drugs are considered the most dangerous, so crimes involving them have the toughest sentences. Possessing or dealing in Class B drugs can also result in a prison sentence or a big fine. Class C drugs are considered slightly less dangerous so the punishment is also slightly less.

Class A
Cocaine and crack • Ecstasy • Heroin
LSD • Magic mushrooms • Opium

Class B
Amphetamines • Cannabis • Ritalin
Codeine • Mephedrone

Class C
Tranquillisers • Some painkillers • Ketamine
Gamma hydroxybutrate (GHB)

▲ Although it is legal to drink alcohol in most countries, alcohol dependence can lead to people becoming homeless and poverty-stricken.

WHO ARE THE CRIMINALS?

Drug users, drug dealers, drug traffickers and drug barons are all involved in drug crime. Some of the profits from selling illegal drugs go towards supporting terrorism or armed conflicts around the world.

The supply chain

Most drug users buy their drugs from a local dealer, or 'pusher'. In turn, these dealers are supplied by a 'wholesaler' who buys large quantities of drugs from drug traffickers. These are the people who smuggle drugs from the place where they are grown or produced to the place where they are sold. Every time a drug changes hands, its price goes up. As the drug is sold on, it is usually mixed, or 'cut' with other ingredients to make it go further. By the time the drug reaches the final user, its cost may have risen by 20 times.

Drug barons

Most of the money stays at the top of the supply chain, making drug barons some of the richest and most powerful people on the planet. A drug baron is the head of an organisation that deals in illegal drugs. His operation is usually known as a drug gang or a drug cartel. Violent feuds can break out between rival drug cartels as they fight for a bigger share in the illegal

drug trade. In October 2009, ten bodies were found in southern Mexico. The victims, members of a drug cartel, had been shot, then cut into pieces, by members of the notorious La Familia, a rival drug cartel. The Mexican government recorded 6,500 drug-related killings in 2009.

▶ *Colombian drug baron Pablo Escobar was ranked 7th richest man in the world in 1989.*

BUSTED!

The Serious Organised Crime Agency (SOCA) published the following statistics for 2008:

90 tonnes of Class A drugs seized in Britain and abroad

60 tonnes of chemicals (used to process narcotics) seized

£46 million of criminal assets confiscated by the courts

756 arrests made in Britain.

▼ *Mexican drug baron Teodoro Garcia Simental was arrested in January 2010 by the Mexican government. A $2.3 m reward had been offered for information leading to his arrest. His drug gang operated in the city of Tijuana, close to the US border. As well as trafficking drugs, it is believed that his gang carried out hundreds of murders in recent years.*

Crime or health problem?

In most countries people who are caught carrying drugs, even small amounts for personal use, are fined or sent to prison. Should drug users be treated as criminals? In June 2009, Antonio Maria Costa, head of the United Nations Office on Drugs and Crime, said: "Law enforcement should shift its focus from drug users to drug traffickers… people who take drugs need medical help, not criminal retribution (punishment)." In the Netherlands, drug addiction is seen as a health issue – addicts are helped to get off drugs rather than put into prison.

THE FLOW OF DRUGS

Illegal drugs are grown on farms, produced in private homes or gardens, or manufactured in secret drug laboratories. However, the bulk of the world's drugs are grown in poorer, developing nations, in wild, inaccessible areas in the mountains or jungle. These areas are difficult to patrol and even if a drug baron is defeated, drug production simply shifts to another part of the world.

Heroin

The 'French Connection' was a drug ring that smuggled heroin from Turkey to France and then onto the United States in the 1960s and 1970s. It was run by the Corsican criminals François Spirito and Antoine Guérini. Opium poppies grown in Turkey were processed in a large factory in the French port of Marseilles. The finished heroin was then shipped in bricks to the United States. The French Connection was finally broken up in the 1970s when Turkey agreed to clamp down on the poppy growers. However, drug gangs in other countries quickly filled the gap in the market. Poppy plants soon began to arrive from the Golden Triangle of Myanmar, Laos and Thailand and the Golden Crescent of Afghanistan, Pakistan and Iran.

▼ *Afghan farmers in a field of opium poppies. Despite considerable efforts by the Afghan government and US coalition forces, opium growing remains the way that many Afghan farmers earn enough money to feed their families.*

FACT FILE

In the 1980s, the Thai government tried to take on the drug barons in the Golden Triangle. In 1983, the Thai army launched an attack against Burmese warlord Khun Sa. He controlled a huge private army and over half of the opium flowing from the Golden Triangle. Though 80 of his men died and his base was destroyed, Khun Sa escaped. US officials promised a $2-million (£1.3-million) reward for his arrest, but Khun Sa did a deal with the government in Myanmar (formerly Burma) and lived near Rangoon until he died in October 2007.

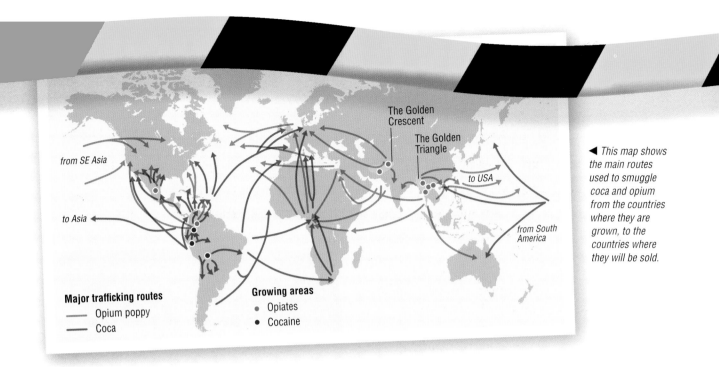

The Golden Crescent

The Golden Triangle

from SE Asia

to Asia

to USA

from South America

◄ This map shows the main routes used to smuggle coca and opium from the countries where they are grown, to the countries where they will be sold.

Major trafficking routes
——— Opium poppy
——— Coca

Growing areas
• Opiates
• Cocaine

Cocaine

Colombian drug cartels began as gangs smuggling jewels and cigarettes who switched to trafficking drugs in the 1970s. Cocaine, a drug derived from the coca plant, became extremely popular in the United States during the 1980s. Soon Colombian drug cartels began to produce it themselves. Colombia became the murder centre of the world as the rival Medellín and Cali cartels fought each other on the streets. Teenage addicts carried out the cartels' dirty work by becoming assassins in a power struggle that claimed some 7,000 lives in just one year.

Ecstasy

Originally developed in 1912 as a potentially life-saving medicinal drug, MDMA, better known as ecstasy, was forgotten about for decades. During the 1970s and 80s secret laboratories began manufacturing ecstasy. It became a popular recreational drug, connected to the rave culture and dance scenes of the 1980s and 90s. It was classified as a Class A drug in the UK in 1977 and became illegal in the USA in 1985. Police now monitor the sale of chemicals needed to produce ecstasy to try to prevent new secret laboratories from being set up.

▶ Ecstasy became linked with the nightclub scene of the 1990s when dancers used the drug to stay alert, yet calm and friendly, as they danced through the night.

THE COST OF DRUGS

Why should the police stop the flow of drugs? Perhaps the main reason is that drugs cost — and not just their street price. As well as harming their own bodies, some drug addicts can damage the lives of everyone around them. Drugs can make people violent and people who take drugs are more likely to commit crime than people who don't.

Addiction and health risks

Drug misuse carries several risks to personal health, including heart attack, panic attack, organ damage, depression and other mental health issues. Drugs such as cocaine and heroin are very addictive: people come to depend on them to feel normal and it takes great willpower to stop taking them. Addicts — people hooked on drugs — have a strong physical need for drugs. As a result, they are sometimes driven by their drug habit to commit crimes, such as burglary or theft, to pay for their next dose, or 'fix'.

▼ Drug addiction can lead to despair for the drug addict and those living in communities blighted by drug misuse.

FACT FILE

Colombia is a country where drugs have had a particularly damaging effect.

- Every year, cocaine causes some 20,000 deaths in Colombia.

- Several hundred thousand Colombians have been forced from their homes by drug barons to make way for coca plantations. Villagers are tortured and killed; rainforests are cut and burnt.

- Every week, Colombian children are blown up by landmines, the weapon of choice for drug traffickers to protect these plantations.

Effect on the community

When there are addicts and drug dealers in a community, it affects everyone else. Neighbourhoods can turn from friendly places into ganglands where people feel helpless and afraid in their own homes. Drugs can ruin lives in other ways. Teenage drug users may drop out of school or waste their lives in prison. Drug-taking parents may lose interest in their children and their babies can be addicted at birth.

▲ *Children affected by Aids watch television at a Thai orphanage. They will have contracted Aids from their parents, who have now died from the disease.*

ON TARGET

In Asia, 30% of HIV/Aids infections are linked to drug use. Some countries, such as Iran, have set up needle exchanges that provide users with clean needles, so they avoid sharing needles with other users who may be infected. However, a recent report revealed that in countries such as China, Malaysia and Thailand, just 1 in 30 drug users have access to such exchanges, which have proved to be one of the most effective ways of preventing the spread of HIV/Aids.

Drugs spread disease

The biggest growth of HIV/Aids outside Africa is within the group of drug users that inject themselves with drugs such as heroin. In the Golden Triangle, one of Asia's two main opium-growing areas (see pages 14–15), there is an Aids epidemic. Drug users in these countries often share needles, helping the rapid spread of the HIV virus that causes Aids. Since the symptoms of Aids can take months or years to develop, the disease spreads through communities to people who have never used drugs, through sexual contact. Health workers are now worried that HIV could spread just as fast in neighbouring India. Hepatitis C, another life-threatening illness, can also be spread by sharing drug needles.

TACKLING THE TRAFFICKERS

The police, the armed forces, intelligence officers, customs officials and coastguards try to stop the flow of drugs within their own country and overseas, where the drugs are often grown and produced. These agents are often up against heavily-armed gangs and may also have to deal with corruption at home and abroad.

The beginning of the chain

The struggle against illegal drugs takes place along the whole route, from the drug pushers in local parks, to the traffickers who bring the drugs into the country and the drug barons who control the supply of drugs. Customs officials work with the police and the military, while intelligence services gather data on individuals, groups and smuggling routes. Ships, helicopters and aircraft patrol the coastline, while coastguards and other units seize many tonnes of drugs from smugglers each year.

▼ *A US Coastguard vessel patrols waters near Mexico on the look-out for drug smugglers.*

Spraying crops

The drugs chain begins with farmers. Raw materials, such as cannabis and coca, are grown on large plantations. Planes, helicopters and satellites are used to spot them from the air, though opium poppies and cannabis plants can be disguised by growing them alongside food crops. In 2003, US-trained Colombian forces used planes to wipe out over 1,000 sq km of coca fields by spraying poisons over them. However, this tactic was heavily criticised as it also punished local farmers and affected the health of innocent local people. Some governments have tried to encourage farmers to grow food crops instead, but it is hard when they can earn as much as 30 times more from the sale of drug crops.

The money trail

Drug gangs often protect themselves by putting the money from drug deals into legal businesses, which is known as money laundering. Drug money is also used to buy property. In some countries, banks and other financial institutions have to inform the police of suspect transactions such as unusually large deposits or transfers of cash. In the UK, any cash deposit of more than £5,000 is automatically flagged up by banks. Any unusual patterns of deposits, often referred to as 'paper trails', are then followed up by the police if they suspect a crime has been committed.

ON TARGET

In the 1970s, military planes and helicopters were used to patrol borders and stop smugglers arriving by air. As a result, air smuggling was greatly reduced. Today, the US Coastguard uses a variety of aircraft, from small planes that can fly low over the water, to Stingray helicopters equipped with machine guns. Aircraft equipped with AWACS – Airborne Warning and Control Systems – can spot smugglers using fast powerboats from 10,000 m up in the air.

▼ *Colombian drug cartel leader Diego Leon Montoya Sanchez was captured during a police operation in southwestern Colombia. Head of the Norte del Valle cartel, it was his gang's money laundering operations that helped lead to his arrest.*

SMUGGLING AND MULES

Drug traffickers use all sorts of methods to smuggle drugs via sea, land and air. Drug couriers, or 'mules', carry drugs in their clothing or luggage, or strap drugs to their bodies. Some swallow packets of drugs, inside condoms or other waterproof packaging, in order to avoid detection.

The land route

Relying on the fact that customs officers will not be able to search every truck that enters or leaves a country, drug smugglers pack illegal drugs into trucks, along with other legal freight. In addition, many land borders stretch for thousands of kilometres, making it perfectly possible for drugs to be smuggled into countries illegally without any intervention from customs officers or other border controls.

▼ *French customs officers search a truck during a routine motorway check. They discovered a huge haul of cocaine.*

Using GPS

Some drug traffickers fit their speedboats with GPS (Global Positioning System). They use the GPS to help them meet up with refuelling ships out at sea, rather than having to come in to land. In addition, GPS is used to keep track of drugs that have been placed in waterproof bales and dropped onto the seabed where they are undetectable by radar. Using GPS, the traffickers know exactly where to pick up the underwater bales.

◀ In 2005 the US Drug Enforcement Agency rescued these puppies from a Colombian drug trafficking gang. They were being used as canine mules to transport packets of liquid heroin to the USA. The packets were surgically implanted inside the puppies.

Air trafficking

Smaller amounts of drugs are carried by air, using hollow objects or small containers with secret compartments. One smuggler disguised himself as a vicar and tried to smuggle in cannabis between the covers of a Bible. Drugs can also be dissolved in water, then transported by soaking clothes in the solution. A sniffer dog at New York's John F Kennedy Airport alerted his handler to drugs which had been absorbed into the fabric of 38 dresses from Bolivia. In some cases, heroin has been mixed into plaster-of-paris and then made into items of crockery.

Drug mules

While some drug couriers are professional criminals, others are individuals bribed to carry out a one-off delivery. Some women mules pretend to be pregnant and use a body suit to hide the drugs. The most notorious mules hide drugs in plastic bags or condoms and swallow them before the journey. It's a risky tactic. In 2006, 40-year-old Nicola Last, from Wales, died after some of the 34 bags of cocaine she had smuggled into Heathrow Airport burst in her stomach, swamping her bloodstream with cocaine. Animals have also been used, such as the puppies shown above.

FACT FILE

The anti-narcotics squad in Madrid, Spain, has made a collection of items used to smuggle drugs, including:

• a bowling ball • bicycles • statuettes
• wheelchairs • tropical fruits • a bottle of shaving cream.

In 2005, a Bahraini man was arrested for carrying oranges filled with heroin. It turned out he was innocent as he had been tricked into carrying the oranges for someone else.

CASE STUDY: BELOW THE WAVES!

Catching drug runners at sea can be like looking for a needle in a haystack. Drug cartels that use sea routes employ all sorts of tactics, from hiding drugs in secret compartments in fishing boats, to using submarines, or sailing hundreds of kilometres off-course, to fool law enforcement agencies.

High-tech transporters

Over the past 15 years, drug gangs have been using homemade submarines to smuggle drugs across national borders. However, in the first six months of 2009, the Colombian Navy managed to seize or destroy 11 of these subs. "Our intelligence is getting better," said Vice-Admiral Jesús Bejarano, commander of Colombia's Pacific fleet. Without a tip-off it's almost impossible to detect these vessels. On the rare occasions that an illegal submarine is detected at sea, crews can open an emergency hatch built into the submarine to sink the vessel and its cargo.

Drug subs!

In June 2009, the Colombian Navy got a tip-off. For eight days, a navy patrol investigated the maze of mangrove swamps in the remote Sanquianga National Park on the Pacific coast. Then — success! Hidden deep in the jungle was a 20-m-long hull in a hangar. This was not your average boatyard. The shipbuilders were applying the final touches to the hull of a submarine. If they hadn't been interrupted, this submarine would have set sail for the United States with up to four tonnes of cocaine on board.

▲ Members of the Colombian Navy guard a homemade submarine in November 2008. When it was captured it contained 1.5 tonnes of cocaine.

FACT FILE

In recent years, Spanish police have noticed a rise in the number of traffickers using jet skis to smuggle drugs into Spain.

- Jet skis can reach speeds of up to 110 km/h, quickly crossing the 12 km Strait of Gibraltar from the Moroccan coast.

- Though small, jet skis can carry up to 50 kg of cannabis.

- If a police boat approaches them, it is easy for drug traffickers to throw the drugs into the water before the police are close enough to inspect them.

Cunning tactics

Small submarines are used to transport as much as a third of all Colombia's cocaine exports. The submarines evade detection by the coastguard and then meet up with high-speed boats, in the middle of the ocean, to pass on the drugs. Anti-drug patrols track all sorts of vessels, from fast speedboats to large container ships. In 2003, the US Coastguard intercepted a freighter carrying 17 tonnes of cocaine, with a total street value of $500 million (£324 million), off the coast of Central America. Traffickers shipping cocaine from South America use more and more cunning or bizarre methods. In 2009 the Mexican Navy discovered a tonne of cocaine hidden inside the frozen carcasses of sharks on board a freight ship.

▼ *A speedboat used by smugglers off the coast of Morocco.*

STOP AND SEARCH

Airports, seaports and border crossings are heavily staffed with security agents on the look-out for drug traffickers. They use X-ray machines and chemical sensors to detect packages hidden in bags or under clothing. But often a drug smuggler's worst enemy comes on four legs — a trained dog can sniff out even small quantities of drugs with its powerful nose.

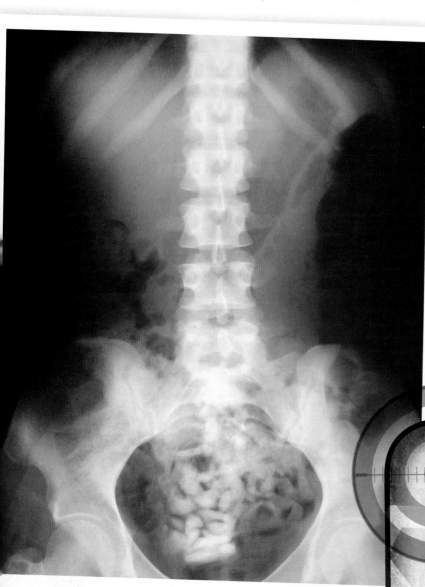

▲ *An X-ray showing a stomach full of drugs wrapped up in condoms.*

Custom control

Customs officers have wide powers: they have the right to stop and search people, vehicles and packages at random. They often rely on tip-offs from other agencies such as the security services. Walk-through X-ray machines 'strip-search' passengers, revealing drugs hidden in clothing. X-ray machines with conveyor belts are used to examine footwear, parcels and baggage. Mobile X-ray vans are also used to inspect cargo. Sometimes robots and video cameras are used to search under vehicles. In dangerous hiding places, such as inside fuel tanks and containers, officers wear safety harnesses and breathing equipment. They carry alarms that warn of toxic fumes.

ON TARGET

Customs officers in the UK are trying out a new system whereby they send X-rays of people suspected of being drug mules straight to the computer screens of X-ray specialists at St Bartholomew's Hospital, London. These X-rays can then be viewed by the experts immediately, rather than wasting time by actually taking the suspects to the hospital's X-ray department.

In the air

Flight crews on planes are also trained to look out for suspicious behaviour. If a passenger looks particularly nervous or is wearing unusually bulky clothing, this could be a disguise. If the passenger seems especially uncomfortable, it could be due to carrying packets of drugs inside the body.

Sense of smell

Handlers who train sniffer dogs say it is impossible to teach a dog how to track down smells any better than it does naturally.

- The secret is to teach it to maintain focus on a single smell and to ignore smells that may otherwise be of greater interest to an untrained dog — such as food!

- Popular breeds for the job are labradors, golden retrievers and German shepherds as they instinctively track by scent.

BUSTED!

One Australian dog sniffed out the drugs hidden in a woman's bra, even though she had smeared coffee, medicines and pepper over it to throw the dog off the scent. In September 1996, a springer spaniel named Jaspar sniffed out 140 kg of cocaine hidden in a cargo of flowers aboard a jumbo jet at Heathrow Airport, London.

- 'Pro-active' dogs are used to sniff out drugs in aircraft, ships' holds and homes.

- 'Passive' dogs are trained to sniff for drugs hidden on people.

▼ *An Italian police sniffer dog searches for drugs in the warehouse of a food shop.*

GLOBAL DRUG WATCH

Intelligence on drug traffickers is gathered by international organisations such as Interpol. They are linked by computer systems to all those involved in fighting the drug trade, including federal agents, local police, border patrols and coastguards. Without such cooperation, it would be hard to track down and convict drug gangs with operations in many different countries.

International cooperation

Interpol (the International Criminal Police Organisation) holds millions of records on international criminals. One specialist wing focuses on drug trafficking, the flow of drugs and smuggling methods. In 2008, Interpol issued more than 3,000 Red Notices, or international wanted person alerts, including one for the Colombian drug baron Daniel Rendon Herrera (see opposite). These resulted in the arrest of more than 700 individuals across the globe. A Red Notice, which includes a photo, can be requested by any Interpol member country. It is then circulated to each of the 188 National Central Bureaux worldwide.

ON TARGET

The European MAOC (Maritime Analysis and Operation Centre-Narcotics) was set up in 2007 with members from seven European countries. Now, if one nation gets intelligence about a shipment of drugs, MAOC officers meet around a table and work out who has the resources to try to intercept it.

▼ *Members of the Mexican Federal Police patrol the city of Culiacan to combat drug trafficking. The Mexican police force works with the National Central Bureau (see above) to support Interpol's international work against drug crime.*

Colombia's most wanted criminal

Daniel Rendon Herrera, a Colombian drug trafficker, was wanted by police for smuggling hundreds of tonnes of cocaine across South America and for his dealings with Mexican drug cartels. He was also wanted in the United States for trafficking cocaine. As a result of Interpol's Red Notice and vital intelligence obtained after seizing computers and hard drives belonging to other drug dealers, the Colombian police closed in on Daniel Rendon Herrera. In April 2009, he was finally captured in a jungle raid involving some 300 anti-drugs police commandos. Rendon had a personal army of up to 1,000 heavily-armed fighters. He offered his gunmen generous cash rewards for each police officer they murdered.

► *Colombian drug trafficker Daniel Rendon Herrera is flanked by Colombian police officers after his arrest in 2009.*

Worldwide strategy

As well as aiding in the arrest of major drug barons, Interpol helps governments by spotting new drug trafficking trends and emerging gangs. Its computer systems translate documents as they are sent, so that reports filed in Spanish in Mexico will appear in English in London. In October 2009, Interpol and the United Nations agreed to become partners to improve the skills of police peacekeepers in troubled areas through training and the sharing of databases containing information about criminals.

SURVEILLANCE

It is hard to follow the trail from a local dealer to the people who run a drug gang, so often the police or customs officers must watch and listen. Tiny cameras and listening devices help to catch gang members making a deal or selling drugs. It takes patience. In September 2009, Spanish police captured the ring leaders of a drug gang from Liverpool, England, but only after months of watching and waiting.

Tracking the criminals

Many different devices are used for surveillance — the art of watching people closely and tracking their movements. Mobile phone records are one helpful way to track criminals, as is CCTV (closed-circuit television). Wiretaps are also useful, being electronic gadgets that allow police officers to listen in to conversations. In April 2005, Australian police used wiretaps to listen in to the activities of an ecstasy drug ring. This led to a police raid on two houses in Melbourne, and they seized 5 million ecstasy tablets and arrested four people.

Hi-tech equipment

Bugs are listening devices used to eavesdrop on conversations. They're so small they can be fitted inside pens or in the bottom of a shoe. Tiny cameras can be fitted in glasses frames to film drug dealers. Another type of camera, a boroscope, is fixed to the end of a flexible rod. It can be used to look around corners and inside plumbing when investigating a gang's hideout or an abandoned drug laboratory. The US DEA was one of the first organisations to put a criminal behind bars thanks to evidence collected by cameras.

▼ CCTV is often used by police to track down drug dealers.

◀ An undercover agent displays the microphone, known as a wire, that will be hidden under his shirt. He will hope to record crucial evidence needed to convict criminals. Early devices, as shown left, were bigger than devices available today.

We're watching you

The war on drugs has given all kinds of governments extra police and military powers. Police and military narcotics units can legally go undercover anywhere and investigate anyone. As a result, there's a danger that secret recordings and photographs can be abused. For example, in June 1972 US President Richard Nixon used members of his anti-drug unit to spy on his enemies in the Watergate Hotel in Washington, DC. It's for this reason that wiretaps and other surveillance can only be carried out with permission from a judge, known as a warrant, in the United States.

ON TARGET

In 2007, the Federal Bureau of Investigation swooped on members of a drug gang based in northern California, USA, as part of Operation Valley Star. A key part of the investigation was an informant who was willing to wear a hidden microphone on his body, known as a wire. He taped a dealer, Mario Diaz, as Diaz discussed the drug gang's operations. Meanwhile an FBI officer took photos and video footage of the meeting.

CASE STUDY:
OPERATION JUNGLEFOWL

Forensic scientists play a vital role in fighting drug crime. Working in laboratories, they use chemical tests to detect small amounts of drugs on clothes, weapons, money and in homes. Some are DNA specialists who are able to link criminals to victims and even to seized drugs. New technology even allows them to trace where the drugs were grown.

Night raid

In 2004, a joint Australian Federal Police (AFD) and customs force lay in wait for a group of traffickers in Western Australia. In the middle of the night, bags were seen being taken off a ship and hidden in bushes near an isolated beach. Each bag was stuffed with blocks of cocaine. Operation Junglefowl sprang into action and officers seized 100 kg of cocaine and arrested three men. To prosecute the smugglers, however, they had to prove the drugs came from overseas.

Back to the lab

AFD scientists then analysed the captured drugs, looking for their chemical fingerprints (DNA). By comparing their results with a large database of samples supplied by the US DEA, they were then able to find out not only what country the cocaine had come from, but even the valley in South America where it was grown. This is because plants grown at different altitudes and on different soils have their own DNA profile.

▼ *A scientist at work in a forensics laboratory.*

What happens in the lab?

In a forensics laboratory, tiny samples, around 5 milligrams, of seized drugs are put into vials and are analysed using microscopes and gas chromatography. They can identify the type of drug, how pure it is and where it came from. The samples are mixed with another substance, called a reagent. This makes the sample separate by colour. For example, in the Van Urk test the presence of LSD makes the sample turn blue.

ON TARGET

The 'shake and vac' machine can find traces of drugs on money or anything else that can be shaken. Particles on the sample fall off and are collected by sucking them up into a machine like a vacuum cleaner. The particles can then be tested. Sometimes a hair or thread found by this method can lead to an arrest, thanks to DNA databases.

◀ The Marquis Reagent test identifies the presence of opiates, codeine or amphetamines in a substance.

BUSTED!

In order to combat drug smuggling, drug dealing and drug abuse in prisons, the governments of several countries have introduced the random drug testing of prisoners. By analysing a urine sample, it is possible to work out whether someone has used illegal drugs recently. Helping someone overcome their drug habit whilst they are in prison could decrease the likelihood of them committing a drug-related crime when they are freed.

GOING UNDERCOVER

Undercover police officers sometimes pose as drug traffickers or drug users to discover links in a drug chain. They may even have to hide their identity from other police officers. Law enforcement agents also work undercover with informants, who may be 'insiders' offering vital information.

Informants

Intelligence operations often have code-names for secrecy, such as Operation Eclectic, which led to the arrest of Howard Marks, a major cannabis trafficker, in 1988. Many investigations depend on informants, people with information about criminal organisations. Why are people willing to inform? Often they are drug users or small-time dealers facing legal charges and the police offer to let them off, providing they can get the drug gang leader convicted.

Working together

Sometimes large teams of undercover police officers work together. DEA officers set out to bust three Mexican and Colombian drug rings. For 10 months from 2004 to 2005, undercover officers were placed along drug transportation routes from Colombia to the US cities where the drugs were sold on the streets. Surveillance was also used to spy on the drug traffickers. The operation led to 164 arrests, the seizure of 1,400 kg of cocaine, 10,000 ecstasy tablets, 97 kg of cannabis, $5.5 million in cash, 58 vehicles and 52 firearms.

▼ *A drug deal takes place on a street corner. Undercover police officers sometimes manage to infiltrate drug dealing operations.*

Moles

Moles are agents or informants working undercover inside a criminal gang. It is very dangerous work – if they are found out, they are likely to be killed. In 2006, an undercover informant, a member of a Hells Angels biker gang, gave information which helped police arrest 27 suspected gang members in Ontario, Canada. The arrests ended an 18-month police operation, named Project Tandem, in which 500 officers investigated drug dealing, murder plans and other crimes.

BUSTED!

In 2005, a school district in Cincinnati, USA, paid a private detective agency $60,000 to have an informant pose as a student for a term and identify all the major drug dealers. In the end, 16 students were arrested. However, critics of the scheme argued that in using an undercover officer, they had tricked the students into breaking the law, which is known as 'entrapment'.

▼ *Members of the Hells Angels motorcycle gang, Ontario branch.*

THE BUST

Raids on drug gangs are often made early in the morning, when gang members are likely to be asleep. Many gangs are heavily armed and the police want to avoid a shoot-out. Just in case, agents often wear bullet-proof vests and are armed themselves. Often raids are carried out at several different addresses at the same time, so gang members have no time to warn each other.

Cocaine factory

Tranquilandia was a large cocaine factory hidden deep in the heart of the Amazon jungle, some 600 km southeast of the Colombian capital of Bogota. Built for Medellín Cartel boss, Pablo Escobar (see photo page 12), it could process around 300 tonnes of cocaine a year. After a tip-off from the US DEA, 40 Colombian policemen in two helicopters and a small plane landed on a nearby airstrip. They found a huge building with 19 laboratories. The police arrested 40 workers and seized almost 14 tonnes of pure cocaine, worth £1 billion.

Cans of ecstasy

A large raid takes good cooperation between large teams combining federal agents, local police, the coastguard and the military. One of the largest ever busts took place in 2008 when Australian police and customs officials seized 4.4 tonnes of ecstasy hidden in a shipping container. The drugs, worth £197 million, were inside 3,000 cans of tomatoes. To track down those behind the shipment, a team of agents carefully opened each tin of tomatoes, removed the drugs and replaced them with harmless tablets. Using wiretaps (see pages 28–29), the police then began to pick up valuable information as the Australian drug gang grew increasingly suspicious of their European suppliers. After a year of watching and waiting, the police swooped and 20 arrests were made at separate addresses.

▲ An Australian police officer displays one of the 3,000 tomato cans packed with ecstasy pills. In all, 15 million ecstasy pills were found in this giant drug haul.

Big busts – good or bad?

A major drug bust is often reported as good news and most people agree it is. However, it is worth considering that a big bust can also lead to further crimes, as big seizures raise the price of drugs. Higher prices mean that addicts must find more money to buy them. The more drugs the police capture and destroy, the more robberies and muggings addicts may commit in order to feed their addiction.

▼ *Afghan and United States DEA Special Agents destroy cannabis bunkers during Operation Albatross (see box right) in Spin Boldak, Kandahar Province, Afghanistan.*

BUSTED!

During Operation Albatross, British Special Boat Service soldiers and local commandos found about £200 million worth of cannabis in trenches and bunkers in Kandahar, Afghanistan in 2008. The drug haul, intended for use by the Taliban to raise funds, was so huge it was estimated to have weighed roughly the same as 30 double-decker buses. The drugs were hidden inside grain sacks and buried in six trenches covering an area the size of two football pitches. They were blown up by RAF Harrier jump jets using three huge bombs.

CASE STUDY: OPERATION HABITAT

After the illegal arms industry, the drug trade is the largest illegal industry in the world. Drug barons in South America and the Golden Triangle in south-east Asia often have their own armies to protect the crops. But very occasionally, the long arm of the law catches up with these criminals.

A rare success

In 2006, a Colombian gang which ran one of the biggest cocaine networks in the UK was finally put behind bars. The two masterminds behind the drug empire, Jesus Anibal Ruiz-Henao and Mario Tascon, were sentenced to 19 and 17 years in prison respectively. It took a four-year investigation, code-named Operation Habitat, to reveal the extent of their drug empire. They admitted bringing 150 kg of cocaine into the UK and sending £19 m back to Colombia. Detectives believe this was only a small fraction of their business.

Breaking the ring

Ruiz-Henao acted as a sort of sales director for large drug cartels based in Colombia. As many as 20,000 people may have worked for the cartel in Colombia. The gang shipped about a tonne of cocaine into the UK each year, usually in trucks or vans. The drugs were hidden in all sorts of ways, from turning them into liquids to smearing packages with mustard or jam to confuse sniffer dogs. Police swooped on the suspects in 2003, 13 years after the gang started. Breaking the drug ring led to 60 arrests and the seizure of 350 kg of cocaine.

▼ This map shows the route used by Ruiz-Henao and Tascon's gang to smuggle cocaine into the UK, and the profits from the business back to Colombia.

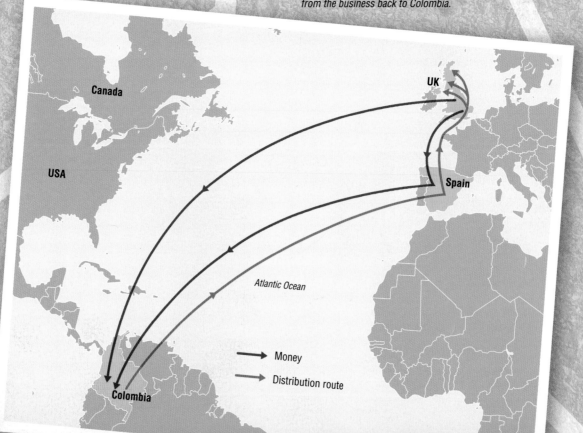

Canada

UK

USA

Spain

Atlantic Ocean

→ Money

→ Distribution route

Colombia

Following the money trail

It can be very difficult to bring drug barons to justice. They employ many people and, especially in drug-growing areas, provide a livelihood to farmers. In addition, in countries like Colombia, they use their wealth to employ the best lawyers and to give out bribes to police forces or juries in order to escape their crimes.

In the case of Operation Habitat, which was a joint operation between the UK National Crime Squad and the Colombian government, the investigation focused on the drug smuggling side of Ruiz-Henao and Tascon's operation. At the same time, Scotland Yard ran Operation Anuric, investigating the money laundering side of their drug business. They managed to discover evidence of the flow of the drug gang's money, as they sent many money transfers in relatively small amounts via Spain or directly to Colombia. They also sent back cash in the same lorries that smuggled the drugs into the UK.

▲ *A Colombian farmer stands in front of his coca plants, the leaves of which are turned into cocaine.*

ON TARGET

In 2006, the UK's Serious Organised Crime Agency (SOCA) began a series of operations against a list of criminal suspects behind a £40bn trade in drugs, corruption and human trafficking. Based in 43 secret locations across Britain, more than 4,000 officers hit the streets, with the power to ban suspects from Britain and seize money made from crime.

REHABILITATION

The USA alone spends about $40 billion each year on trying to disrupt the flow of illegal drugs. It also arrests 1.5 million of its citizens each year for drug offences, most just for possession. Despite this, the flow of drugs continues. Some countries are now focusing attention on trying to reduce the demand for drugs, through drug rehabilitation programmes.

What should be done?

In June 2009, Antonio Mario Costa, head of the United Nations Office on Drugs and Crime, spoke of the need to treat drug use as an illness rather than a crime. Since people with drug addiction provide most of the demand for illegal drugs, treating their problems is one of the best ways to shrink the illegal drug industry. He encouraged police forces around the world to focus their attention on the small number of people who commit the most serious and violent drug-related crimes, rather than on the large number of drug users. In addition, he suggested that if governments were to improve the housing, education and other public services in poorer communities, it would make people less likely to take up drugs.

▼ *Mealtime for visitors to the drug rehabilitation programme at Thankrabok Monastery in Thailand. The monastery runs a tough, but successful, drug detox programme to help addicts withdraw from drugs.*

Treatment

Drug treatment schemes not only help people to give up drugs but also help them to take back control of their lives. Some heroin addicts may need to be prescribed methadone, a heroin-replacement drug, to help them come off heroin. Others need a short hospital admission to help them withdraw from drugs. Rehabilitation clinics range from luxury places where wealthy people go to help them with their drug problems, to day centres running a range of courses or therapy sessions. Counselling and group therapy are a mainstay of drug rehabilitation programmes, giving people ideas on how to stay off drugs and solve other problems in their lives. Recovering addicts may be given help to find a home, or be given skills training to get a job.

▲ Recovering drug addicts talk about their problems at an addiction treatment centre in a suburb of Mexico City, Mexico.

ON TARGET

Some countries have a harsh approach to tackling drugs. Under Chinese law, users of illegal drugs can be locked up in drug rehabilitation centres, sometimes for years. Here they are forced to work and take exercise in a harsh, prison-like environment, as well as receiving drug re-education. Meanwhile, people caught drug dealing in China can be punished by the death sentence and are executed.

◄ Anti-drug education for the inmates of the Kunming Municipal Compulsory Rehabilitation Centre in China (see above).

THE FUTURE

Drug crime will remain an international problem for many years to come. Law enforcement agencies will continue to try to stop the flow of drugs into their own country and across national borders. Some experts believe that education programmes are an important tool in the fight against drug crime. Others continue to debate whether legalising cannabis would decrease drug crime.

Legalise cannabis?

Some people believe that legalising cannabis will stop money getting into the hands of criminal gangs. It will also keep young people away from criminals and help control the type of cannabis available. Others believe that when someone experiments with cannabis this can be a stepping stone towards using more addictive drugs. In addition, the type of cannabis available today is far stronger than in the past, and there is a link between this and more people developing mental health problems.

The Dutch approach

In the Netherlands, Dutch law divides drugs into addictive 'hard' drugs, such as cocaine and heroin, and 'soft' drugs, such as cannabis, which are less addictive. For many years, using cannabis has been tolerated by the Dutch police. The government allows a small number of coffee houses to sell small quantities of cannabis for personal use to people over the age of 18. The aim is to create a safe environment for cannabis users to buy and use cannabis and to keep them away from drug dealers.

▶ The sign outside a Dutch coffee house which is allowed to sell small amounts of cannabis.

Drug use prevention

Many governments spend money on drug prevention schemes. These include drug education in schools or at other events attended by young people. Through teaching young people about the effects of different drugs, the health risks and possible outcomes of adopting a drug lifestyle, they become more able to make an informed choice about whether to try drugs or not in the future. Former drug users or addicts will often tell their life stories to the pupils, as an example of what can happen if you adopt a drug user's lifestyle.

▲ *Here young people are learning how to recognise different illegal drugs at a drug awareness event in London.*

The future

Drug specialists, academics, health professionals and politicians continue to research the links between drug use and crime, and think about how to treat addiction and prevent people from becoming involved with drugs. It may be possible to develop a vaccine against certain addictive drugs but this could create a debate about who should receive it. And new drugs may be developed that will bring a fresh set of problems with them.

FACT FILE

Most governments will continue to label certain drugs as illegal and allow others to remain on the right side of the law. At the moment drugs that improve academic performance, so called 'smart' drugs that make people's brains work faster or smarter, are legal. This doesn't mean that it is the right thing to take such drugs, as it could be seen as a form of cheating. Performance enhancing drugs in sport have been banned for many years.

GLOSSARY

Addiction When someone has a strong physical need for something, such as a drug or a pastime.

Amphetamine A powerful drug which stimulates the brain. Also known as 'speed'.

Cannabis A sedative drug made from the dried leaves of the cannabis plant.

Cocaine A powerful and addictive drug made from the leaves of the coca plant.

Customs officer A government employee who monitors the flow of goods into the country, in order to detect any illegal activity, whether carried on a traveller, in their luggage or in freight.

DEA (Drug Enforcement Administration) Part of the US Department of Justice, this law enforcement agency combats drug crime in all its forms.

DNA (deoxyribonucleic acid) The main molecule that holds genetic information.

Drug baron The leader of a powerful drug gang.

Drug cartel A large criminal organisation that produces and smuggles drugs.

Ecstasy The common name for MDMA, a type of amphetamine often linked to the dance club scene.

FBI (Federal Bureau of Investigation) US government security service responsible for investigating crimes.

Forensics Using science to solve crimes.

Gas chromotography A scientific method used to separate out the different chemicals in a substance.

Heroin A very addictive drug made from morphine, a chemical found in opium.

HIV/Aids HIV stands for the human immunodeficiency virus, which leads to Aids (Acquired Immune Deficiency Syndrome).

Intelligence Police officers use the word 'intelligence' to refer to the gathering of information that may lead to solving or preventing a crime.

Interpol (International Criminal Police Organisation) An international agency that helps police forces from different countries work together and share information.

LSD (Lysergic acid diethylamide) A powerful hypnotic drug commonly known as 'acid'.

Mole A spy or informant working inside an organisation.

Money laundering Hiding the source of illegally-made money by investing in legal businesses or moving it from one bank account to another.

Mule Someone who smuggles illegal drugs, often inside their body.

Narcotics Sleep-inducing drugs, including heroin, morphine and other opiates.

Opium An addictive drug made from the seeds of a type of poppy. Opiates are drugs prepared from opium, such as heroin, morphine and codeine.

Pusher An illegal seller of drugs.

Rehabilitation To enable someone to return to a normal life, especially after they have been disabled or become addicted to drugs or alcohol.

Sniffer dog A police dog trained to sniff out illegal goods, such as drugs or explosives.

Trafficking Smuggling illegal goods, especially drugs.

FURTHER INFORMATION

Books

Nathaniel Harris, *What if we do nothing?: Drug Trafficking*, Franklin Watts, 2009

Clive Gifford, *Crimebusters: How Science Fights Crime*, OUP, 2007

Chris Cooper, *Forensic Science*, Dorling Kindersley, 2008

P Saunders/S Myers, *Choices and Decisions: Taking Drugs*, Franklin Watts, 2004

Jacqui Bailey, *Talk About Drugs*, Wayland, 2008

Sean Connolly, *Straight Talking About Drugs*, Franklin Watts, 2006

Websites

Sites relating to the fight against drug crime.

www.drugs.homeoffice.gov.uk
Up-to-date information about the UK Home Office's efforts to tackle illegal drugs.

www.drugscope.org.uk
This website provides information about drugs, the latest research and links to treatment centres nationwide, as well as D-World, a separate section of their website designed for 11-14-year olds.

www.drugwarfacts.org
An online book packed with useful information about illegal drugs as well as useful statistics for further study.

www.justice.gov/dea/concern/concern.htm
Part of the US Drug Enforcement Administration's website giving detailed information about illegal drugs.

www.soca.gov.uk
The website of the UK's Serious Organised Crime Agency, with information about the latest threats and solved crimes.

www.unodc.org
The United Nations' Office on Drugs and Crime website, with information on drug control and crime prevention.

Sites offering education, advice or help.

www.abovetheinfluence.com
US website for young people, providing information, videos, games and quizzes about illegal drugs.

www.pada.org.uk
The website of Parents Against Drug Abuse, an organisation that supports the families of drug users.

www.talktofrank.com
This website has a useful A-Z of drugs, detailing the effects and legal position as it relates to individual drugs. Also has advice on how to get help with a drug problem.

www.teenissues.co.uk/AlcoholAndDrugs.html
An online essay about alcohol and drugs, written for teenagers.

www.thesite.org/drinkanddrugs
This website is aimed at young people and gives masses of information about drugs, their effects and the legal position.

Australia

www.adin.com.au/content.asp?Document_ID=71
This part of the website of the Australian Drug Information Network provides links to alcohol and drug services for young people across Australia.

www.cyh.com/HealthTopics/HealthTopicCategories.aspx?p=163
This part of South Australia's Children, Youth and Women's Health Service is dedicated to providing information about drugs and alcohol, and is aimed at teenagers.

Note to parents and teachers: every effort has been made by the Publishers to ensure that these websites are suitable for children, that they are of the highest educational value, and that they contain no inappropriate or offensive material. However, because of the nature of the Internet, it is impossible to guarantee that the contents of these sites will not be altered. We strongly advise that Internet access is supervised by a responsible adult.

INDEX

addicts, drug 9, 13, 15, 16-17, 31, 35,
    treatment for habit 31, 38-41
Afghanistan 14, 35
alcohol 8, 10, 11
amphetamines 8, 9, 11
Australia 25, 28, 30, 34

barons, drug 12, 13, 14, 16, 18, 26, 27, 36, 37
Bolivia 21
Brazil 9
bugs, listening 28

Canada 33, 41
cannabis 8, 9, 11, 18, 21, 32, 35, 40
    legalise 9, 40
cartels, drug 12, 15, 19, 22, 27, 34, 36
China 17, 39
CCTV 28
coastguard 18, 19, 23, 26, 34
cocaine (coca) 8, 9, 10, 11, 15, 16, 18, 20, 21, 22, 23, 27,
    30, 32, 34, 36, 37, 40
Colombia 8, 12, 15, 16, 18, 19, 21, 22, 23, 26, 27, 32, 34,
    36, 37
Costa, Antonio Maria 13, 38
couriers, drug 20-21
customs officers 18, 20, 24, 28, 30

dealers, drug 12-13, 16, 18, 27, 28, 29, 32, 33, 36, 37, 39
DNA 30, 31
dogs, sniffer 21, 24, 25, 36
DEA 21, 28, 30, 32, 34, 35
drugs,
    classification of 11, 13, 15
    education 40-41
    legalising 9, 40-41
    possession of 8, 11, 38
    production of 8, 12, 14-15, 18,
    'smart' 41
    smuggling 8, 12, 15, 18-27, 30, 31, 36-37
    trafficking 8, 12, 13, 15, 18-27, 30, 32, 36, 37
    types of 8, 10-11, 14

ecstasy 9, 10, 11, 15, 28, 32, 34
Escobar, Pablo 12, 34
European MAOC 26

FBI 29
forensics 30, 31
France 14, 20
French Connection 14

gangs, drug 8, 9, 12, 13, 14, 15, 16, 19, 21, 26, 28, 29, 32,
    33, 34, 36, 37, 40
Garcia Simental, Teodoro 13
Golden Crescent 14, 15
Golden Triangle 14, 15, 17, 36
Guérini, Antoine 14

heroin 8, 9, 10, 11, 14, 16, 17, 21, 31, 39, 40
HIV/Aids 17

informants 29, 32, 33
intelligence, police 18, 26-27, 32
Interpol 26, 27
Iran 14, 17

Khun Sa 14

Laos 14, 17
LSD 11, 31

Marks, Howard 32
Mexico 12, 13, 18, 23, 26, 27, 32, 39
money laundering 19, 37
Montoya Sanchez, Diego Leon 19
mules 20-21, 24
Myanmar 14, 17

Netherlands 13, 40
Nixon, President Richard 9, 29

Operation Albatross 35
Operation Anuric 37
Operation Eclectic 32
Operation Habitat 36-37
Operation Junglefowl 30
Operation Valley Star 29
opium 9, 11, 14, 15, 17, 18

Pakistan 14
police 9, 14, 15, 16, 18, 19, 23, 26-27, 28, 29, 32, 34, 36,
    37, 38, 40, 41
    undercover work 28, 29, 32-33, 37
prisons 13, 16, 31
pushers 12, 18

rehabilitation 38-39
Rendon Herrera, Daniel 26, 27
Ruiz-Henao, Jesus Anibal 36, 37

SOCA 13, 37
Spain 21, 23, 28, 37
Spirito, Francois 14
submarines 22-23
surveillance 28-29, 32

Tascon, Mario 36, 37
terrorism 12
Thailand 14, 17, 38
tobacco 8, 10
Turkey 14

UK 10, 11, 13, 15, 19, 21, 24, 25, 27, 36, 37,
UNDOC 9, 13, 27, 38
USA 9, 10, 14, 15, 18, 19, 21, 22, 23, 27, 28, 29, 32, 33, 38

wires (microphones) 29
wiretaps 28, 29, 34

X-rays 24

SERIES CONTENTS

Cybercrime Hacking • Case study: Gary McKinnon • Phishing • Cyberbullying • Cyberstalking • Virus attacks • Malware • Social networking sites • Fraudulent websites • Denial-of-service attacks • Identity theft • Case study: Pirate Bay • Cyberterrorism • Cyberwars • Case study: Cyberwars in Eastern Europe • Cybersecurity

Drug crime Worldwide drug problem • Which drugs are illegal? • Who are the criminals? • The flow of drugs • The cost of drugs • Tackling the traffickers • Smuggling and mules • Below the waves • Stop and search • Global drug watch Surveillance • Operation Junglefowl • Going undercover • Drug bust • Operation Habitat • Drugs on the street • The future of drug crime

Forensics The use of forensics • The history • Securing the crime scene • Using post-mortems • Looking at the evidence: insects • Soil and seeds • Blood • DNA evidence • Bones and skulls • Clothes and shoes • Forgeries • Guns and bullets • Narcotics • Crash investigations • Explosions • Forensics and ancient history

People trafficking Defining people trafficking • History of people trafficking • The traffickers • The victims • Forced labour • The sex industry • Trafficking children • Source countries • In transit • Border controls • Case study: The European Union • Catching the criminals • Loopholes in the law • Police and welfare • Working with NGOs • Raising awareness • Taking a stand

Gun crime Defining gun crime • Which guns are used? • Who commits gun crime? • Case study: killing spree • How much gun crime is there? • Gun dealing • Gun control • Arming the police • Case study: Ganglands • Solving gun crime • Firearms in the crime lab • Case study: Washington snipers • Combating gun crime • Operation Trident • Gun crime in the media • Firearms debate

Youth crime The history of youth crime • The nature of youth crime • The criminals • The age of criminal responsibility • Social deprivation • The youth justice system • Punishment or rehabilitation • Case studies • Gang culture • Anti-social behaviour • Alcohol and drugs • Cybercrime • Combating the problem • The future

Kidnapping and piracy Explaining kidnapping and piracy • The history of kidnapping and piracy • The motives: Lindbergh Case • Terry Waite • Kidnapping during war • Surviving a kidnap or act of piracy • Commercial piracy • Combating kidnaps and acts of piracy • The future

Policing and justice How legal systems work • How policing works • The history of police forces • Aims of the criminal justice system • Human rights issues • The power of the police • Neighbourhood policing • Do victims get a fair deal? • Racism in police force • Youth justice • Combating terrorism • The police force of the future